Dog Training

A Detailed Dog Book For A Well Trained, Obedient Dog

© **Copyright 2014 - All rights reserved.**

This document is geared towards providing exact and reliable information in regards to the topic and issue covered. The publication is sold with the idea that the publisher is not required to render accounting, officially permitted, or otherwise, qualified services. If advice is necessary, legal or professional, a practiced individual in the profession should be ordered.

- From a Declaration of Principles which was accepted and approved equally by a Committee of the American Bar Association and a Committee of Publishers and Associations.

In no way is it legal to reproduce, duplicate, or transmit any part of this document in either electronic means or in printed format. Recording of this publication is strictly prohibited and any storage of this document is not allowed unless with written permission from the publisher. All rights reserved.

The information provided herein is stated to be truthful and consistent, in that any liability, in terms of inattention or otherwise, by any usage or abuse of any policies, processes, or directions contained within is the solitary and utter responsibility of the recipient reader. Under no circumstances will any legal responsibility or blame be held against the publisher for any reparation, damages, or monetary loss due to the information herein, either directly or indirectly.

Respective authors own all copyrights not held by the publisher.

The information herein is offered for informational purposes solely, and is universal as so. The presentation of the information is without contract or any type of guarantee assurance.

The trademarks that are used are without any consent, and the publication of the trademark is without permission or backing by the trademark owner. All trademarks and brands within this book are for clarifying purposes only and are the owned by the owners themselves, not affiliated with this document.

Table of Contents

Introduction 1
Food Aggression 3
Over-protectiveness 7
Excessive Barking 9
Feigning Deafness 11
Not Housetrained 13
Pulling on Lead 15
Jumping on People 17
Puppy Biting 19
Chewing Everything 21
Separation Anxiety 23
Bonus Tips 25
Conclusion 27

Introduction

I want to thank you and congratulate you for purchasing the book, *"Dog Training: A Detailed Dog Book For A Well Trained, Obedient Dog"*.

Have you and your furry little friend been having some problems in the area of discipline and training? Do you need some help on the issue? Or do you want to train your little adorable puppy to make him or her a perfect friend? Are you looking for a way to make the learning process fast, easy and reliable? Are you tired of dog training programs that seem incomplete because they only cover how to teach dog basic commands while leaving out the important issues that you could be facing like food aggression, excessive barking, over-protectiveness, pulling the lead and even jumping on people? This book seeks to unravel what works in getting your dog to stop those annoying habits and start embracing good habits that you will certainly want to brag about.

You will also get to learn about various things that you could probably be doing innocently that could be fuelling your dog's or puppy's bad behaviour. If you are looking for a book that will transform the way you unleash the most desirable characteristics in your dog, then this book is certainly what you are looking for. By reading this book, you will get to learn ten of the most common problems that dog owners experience and how to deal with each of them so that you get the best from your dog.

Training your dog has never been easier thanks to this book, as you will get to learn how to deal with:

- Food aggression
- Over protectiveness
- Excessive barking
- Feigning Deafness
- Pulling on lead
- Jumping up on people
- Separation Anxiety
- Puppy Biting
- Chewing everything

-Not being house trained

-And much! much! More!

You can rest assured that this book will mark the end of some of the annoying tendencies or behaviours that your dog or puppy has been showing for a while.

Thanks again for purchasing this book, I hope you enjoy it!

Food Aggression

This occurs when a dog is highly protective of its food and considers anyone who approaches his food bowl a threat to his vital food resource. A dog displaying signs of food aggression will snarl, growl, glare at you and position himself (or herself) between you and the food; these behaviors will increase in intensity the closer anyone gets to his food bowl. If this behavior is not corrected, it may even escalate and the dog may start showing his aggressive guarding behaviour over his toys, the part of the room that he likes or he may even take over your bed and start growling at you if you dare approach it. If your dog has this tendency, you ought to rectify it properly. So, how do you deal with the problem?

Treating Puppy Food Aggression

This type of food aggression is the easiest type to cure if it is dealt with early enough and if consistent behaviour modification exercises are applied.

Method 1: Hand feeding

One method you should consider is hand feeding the dog regularly. Your puppy will learn that the human hand is good thing and that delicious treats come from it. Hand feeding the dog will also strengthen the bond between you and your puppy, as he will soon realize that your hand approaching him during feeding time is something to be welcomed and not something to be feared. Finally, this training method establishes who the leader of the dog-owner relationship is, as you set the pace of feeding and you can give him certain commands, such as 'sit' before he gets any food. This practice should be encouraged throughout the dog's lifetime, as it encourages bite inhibition.

Method 2: Stroke the dog regularly

You should also try to pet and stroke the puppy regularly when he is eating and talk to him or her in a soothing voice. This also shows the puppy that you are not a threat to his food.

Method 3: The magic wand

Another method to try that will really amuse your puppy/dog is the magic hand. When your puppy is eating from his bowl, quickly dip your hand in it and then feed him (with the same hand) with something much tastier than what he had in his bowl. Quickly remove your hand after doing this. After your puppy enjoys that little treat, sniffs around in his bowl to see if he finds anymore of that tasty treat and then finally resumes eating, dip your hand in again and repeat the procedure. This exercise discourages food aggressive behavior because your puppy will now welcome your hand in his bowl and associate it with tasty treats; therefore, he will not see it as a threat to his food.

Method 4

Another tactic that you should try is this: every time you walk close to your puppy's food while he is eating, toss in something tasty in his bowl. In fact, this exercise will be more effective if every member of the family practices this. Your puppy will quickly associate people who come near to his bowl as bearers of sweet treats and hence not a threat to his food.

Treating dog to dog food aggression

This type of behaviour is also a common form of dog aggression and it should not be encouraged in any way. If all other tactics fail, you should let the dogs eat apart to stop the food aggression altogether.

Treating food aggression in grown up dogs

Method 1

First, you should always stand at a distance that your food-aggressive dog is comfortable with and then gradually decrease this distance over time. He will soon realize that you really are not a threat to his food.

Method 2

You should also ensure that there are no objects or foods that he loves dearly just lying around. This kind of activity encourages food aggression in dogs and should be discouraged. That also means that you should not constantly have food in your dog's bowl all the time. It is also important to note that feeding the dog highly palatable foods may encourage food aggression so you should stop this practice.

Method 3

One method you could try to discourage food aggression in grown up dogs is to lessen the amount of food you always put in your dog's food bowl by a great amount. Once he has gobbled up all of the food, he will still want more and will practically beg you to come near to his food bowl to give him some more food. You can then put some more into his bowl and once he has eaten that up, he will still want some more. Repeat the exercise about once a week and soon your dog will love having you near his food bowl.

Over-Protectiveness

The name says it all. Overprotectiveness occurs when a dog guards its owner like a prized possession whenever other animals or humans get near its owner. The dog is very territorial and therefore will bark, growl, get between its owner and the other person and even lounge and bite when someone approaches.

Many things may cause such overprotective behaviour. For instance, you might have considered this type of behavior cute when the dog was a puppy, which means that the puppy was encouraged to continue his or her behavior. In this case, the dog grew up believing that this type of behaviour is acceptable. The dog may also be scared of new people so the idea of being aggressive is to attempt to defend itself and its owner. The dog may also sense fear in the owner or the owner may be portraying a submissive energy making the dog to feel the need to 'step up' and be the alpha male that protects the owner.

Before you can try to solve the problem of over-protectiveness in your dog, you have to first determine why he is displaying such aggression in the first place. If it is that he is nervous when visitors come over to your house, then you should keep him close to you when visitors come by and calmly reassure him that you are fine and that everything is all right. If he growls when a visitor comes by then you should firmly tell him "no" or some other word that you use to show your disapproval. He should also be praised and rewarded when he shows proper social behaviour when visitors arrive; consider giving him a treat when he behaves or have the visitor throw him his favourite snack. Do not let the visitors touch him if he shows any signs of fear.

You should try to be calm and collected when you have visitors over. If your dog senses your fear, he will want to take over and want to defend you. So try to be calm when you have visitors over and your dog will see that you are fine; this way, you will make him to relax.

If you have an overprotective dog, you should let him socialize as much as possible in controlled social interactions. So take him out on walks. You may want to walk with him alone for the first couple of walks and then gradually have more and more people walk with you. This will help to make the dog get used to having a number of people around and hence lessen his overprotective streak.

Excessive Barking

Dogs bark for a number of reasons. To understand the reasons for excessive barking, we have to take a deeper look into the reasons why dogs bark and then come up with useful ways of decreasing the tendency of the dog to bark excessively.

Why dogs bark

Excitement

Some dogs get very excited during playtime and then start to bark non-stop. If this occurs, simply slow down the pace of the game and allow him to calm down. If he continues to bark, stop the game play altogether and tell him firmly to "stop barking" or some other command that you will only use when you want him to stop barking. When he does stop barking, praise him and give him a treat too.

Boredom/loneliness

Many dogs also bark out of boredom or loneliness. You should ensure that your dog always has something to do or that he always has some toy he can play with to keep him occupied and keep this type of excessive barking at bay.

To seek attention

Many dogs just bark as a means of seeking attention. When your dog was a puppy, it is very likely that he used to bark excessively to get your attention and was always successful in doing so. Hence, you inadvertently reinforced this kind of behaviour and it is this behaviour that he has taken with him into adulthood that is causing such problems. If your dog is barking excessively as a means to get your attention and you are sure that there is nothing else wrong with him, simply ignore him. After a while, he will realize that the excessive barking is not getting him anywhere so he will stop.

Fear

Some dogs bark when they are fearful. To curb this type of behaviour, you must first teach your dog to be obedient and to look to you for his behavior cues and relax. You can then start training him in controlled social situations where people approach him from far off. If he remains relaxed, give him a treat and praise him. Over the next couple of weeks, have people come closer and closer, only to the point where he remains relaxed. Continue praising him and giving him his treat when he remains composed. When he starts allowing people to come really close, you can have them throw him his favourite treats so that he starts associating people with those treats; this will help to lessen his fear of people.

To warn or alert people

Most dogs also bark to warn or alert us of something suspicious. Though this is a good trait, it becomes annoying when the dog continues barking without ceasing. To correct this, you need to signal to the dog after he has barked once or twice that he was good for alerting you but now you have the situation under control and he should stop. Teaching him 'enough' will do the trick. When he starts the barking, do something to get his attention (he will momentarily stop the barking) and tell him in a firm voice "enough." If he remains quiet, immediately give him a treat and praise him but ensure that you do not give him the treat while he is barking because he will feel that he is being praised for barking and not for keeping quiet. Repeat this exercise as often as possible until the dog completely understands the command *enough* and responds to it positively.

As you can see, training your puppy from a tender age that excessive barking is wrong will lessen the likelihood of him developing the habit in adulthood. Hence, teach him the command *enough* as early as possible and do not encourage him to bark at people for extended periods. Also, you should get him used to the sounds of common household objects, such as vacuum cleaners, hair dryers etc. so that he does not become fearful when he hears these sounds.

Feigning Deafness

When you tell your dog to do something and he does not respond, you may think that he is being disobedient and you may want to punish him for this. However, you might be forgetting one very important thing about dogs when you do this; dogs do not speak English and so there will definitely be language barriers to communication between the both of you.

It may be that your dog simply does not understand you. You cannot expect to just get up one day and tell your dog a new command and expect that he will understand you. You have to teach him these commands, preferably when he is still a puppy and then use positive reinforcement to ensure that the correct response to your spoken command gets followed and encouraged.

When teaching commands, it is best to use short and simple words combined with hand gestures. You should also praise your puppy or give him a treat whenever he responds correctly to the command that you are teaching.

Never hit or shout at your puppy when he does not respond correctly as this may instill fear in the puppy and create a different kind of problem all together. This will also foster a relationship of fear and distrust between you and your puppy, which is definitely not the kind of relationship you will want to have.

You should also be consistent in your command words. For instance, do not use "stop" one instance when you want him to stop barking and then use "no" at another time. This will only confuse your puppy and you will not get the response you desire.

Your dog may also not respond to your command because your tone does not match your command. For example, if when you arrive at home and your dog named Kit jumps on you and starts licking you from head to toe and you say "stop Kit, stop" in a playful tone whilst giggling and pushing Kit gently, then in effect, you have just communicated to Kit that "Stop Kit, stop" means "this is a fun game, lets continue playing." You have to ensure that your tone matches the command. If you want Kit to stop, say firmly "Stop Kit, stop."

It may also be that your dog understands very well what you are telling him to do but he has chosen to ignore the command. Remember that dogs are pack animals and there is always one leader, or alpha male who is the head of them all. In the situation where your dog is ignoring you, he considers himself the leader in the relationship; therefore, you have to take steps to re-establish yourself as the dominant one in the relationship.

Not Housetrained

Housetraining your dog or puppy calls for patience, vigilance, commitment and most important of all, consistency. Before you start your training, you should expect that almost every dog will have an accident in the house. He may even have more than one accident; it just comes with living with a canine. If an accident happens, ensure that you clean it up completely using the required chemicals, so that no more odours of the waste remain there. The dog will be more likely to pass waste there again if it can smell the scent of its waste in the area. Always remember that the more consistent you are with your housetraining, the faster your dog or puppy will learn the acceptable behaviours.

You should try to establish and maintain a routine in your dog's life and let him understand that there is a time to eat, a time to play and a time to use the potty. You should put your puppy on a regular feeding schedule so that he will eliminate at about the same time each day too; this will make housetraining easier for both of you. Take your puppy outside frequently (at least every two hours and immediately after eating, drinking and after he wakes up) and pick one bathroom spot outside. Always take your dog to that spot on a leash and while your puppy is eliminating, use commands like "go potty" that he will eventually learn to associate with the act of eliminating. You should also reward your puppy every time he eliminates outdoors and responds positively to the "go potty" command. Do ensure that you give your puppy the treat immediately after he eliminates and not after she goes back inside the house.

Generally speaking, a puppy can control his bladder for around an hour for each month of age. So if your puppy is two months old, he can only hold it in for around two hours so ensure that you don't exceed the two hours between bathroom breaks or you will surely have an accident. In case you have to spend several hours outside the home, you will need to use the services of a dog walker to ensure that your puppy has his bathroom breaks. You should also pick up your puppy's water dish about two to three hours before it is time for him to go to bed. This will reduce the chance of him wanting to pass waste during the night because most puppies can sleep for a maximum of seven hours without having to eliminate.

You should also supervise your puppy when he is indoors and take him out to his designated spot for elimination whenever you see him showing the signs that he wants to eliminate. These signs include restlessness, scratching the floor, squatting or sniffing around.

When you are unable to supervise your puppy for short periods, restrict him to areas that are too small for him to pass waste in. The puppy should be able to stand, turn around and lie down but it should not be so big that he can pass waste there.

Pulling On Lead

Keeping your dog under control when you go out on walks is a problem for many dog owners and because of this, many dog owners limit the number of walks they take with their dogs each month. This can be detrimental to the health of the relationship because such walks help to increase the bond between the dog and its owner. So, what can you do to control an unruly dog?

Well the first step that every unruly dog owner must take is to start looking at his or her own body language and the energy that they communicate while walking their dogs. Is it a message of leadership that says "I am the alpha in this dog-owner relationship"? You would be surprised at the results that walking with proper posture and with confidence while giving a dog a stroll can have on the overall behaviour of your dog; so try to lead with confidence.

You should also consider filming the walk to see your behavior and how you respond to your dog. Are you putting undue tension on the dog leash or walking with bad posture? How do you react when your dog starts pulling? These are all essential questions and the answers from these may help you pinpoint trouble points along the walk. In doing so, you will therefore be able to take the necessary steps to fix these problems.

You should also consider using a short dog leash with a collar that is positioned at the top of the head. When you place your dog collar nearer to the bottom part of the dog's neck, you are actually helping your dog to pull you along because the lower part of the neck is where most of the dog's power is located. The upper part of the neck is more of a sensitive area so your dog will be less likely to pull you when its collar is positioned there. Short leashes also give you much more control over your dog than longer leases, so use them as opposed to using the longer ones.

You should walk in front of your dog during walks. This will send a message to him of who the leader in the relationship is and therefore he will be much more compliant and receptive to your commands.

Lastly, you should practise the walk regularly even if your dog behaves badly during the first couple of trials. The more you practise, the more your dog will learn what is expected of him and what you do not like. There will be no improvement if both of you do not go out there and practise the walk, so give it a try as often as possible. You will be surprised at how quickly visible changes in the quality of your walk will take place if you try harder and practice as often as possible. In addition, consider giving your dog a treat whenever he behaves properly on the walk as an incentive to keep him going and encourage the good behaviour.

Jumping on People

When dogs meet, they usually greet each other by sniffing each other's faces. When they try to jump on you and lick your face, that is exactly what they are trying to do. Although this practice may be cute in puppyhood, it can become quite annoying and possibly dangerous in adulthood. Imagine having a 120 pound German shepherd jumping up on you or your toddler or elder in a bid to greet you! This could cause a lot of damage to those involved. Therefore, when you see that your puppy has this tendency to jump on people, you should try curbing it before it gets worse and becomes a full-blown problem in the dog's adult life.

Since dogs usually jump on you out of excitement and as a means of greeting you, you have to let him know that you will only greet him when his paws are on the ground. Your touch and your attention are the cues that you will use to let the dog know when he is doing something good.

Therefore, you should ignore the dog when his paws are not grounded; do not give him any attention at all when he tries to prance on you. Just stand straight up and look over his head. If he continues to jump on you, do not make any sound and turn away. The instance his paws become grounded, greet him with the love and affection that he craves and if he jumps on you during this point, begin ignoring him again until his paws are on the ground.

When you only give him the attention he craves when his feet are grounded, he will learn what is expected of him and over time, this tendency to jump on people when greeting them will decrease. Ensure that you start greeting him as soon as his feet touch the ground; he will soon make the connection that only when his paws are grounded will he get the love and affection that he craves.

If your enter a room and your dog immediately jumps on you, simply step back outside and pull up the door behind you but do not close it. Through the crack say "sit" and then calmly walk back into the room and greet him calmly. Remember that your dog is able to pick up on your spirit, so try to portray one that is calm and collected. If he or she jumps on you again, simply step back outside and repeat the procedure. Once she has learnt what is expected of him or her, have your friends and family practice the exercise with him or her; tell them the procedure and exactly how your dog should behave. You know what they say: *"Practice makes perfect.";* the more you practice, the better your dog will become at losing those behavioral problems and becoming a better dog.

Puppy Biting

A bite is one of the many different forms of communication used by puppies. It is normal for puppies to bite; actually, they should be allowed to experiment with biting so that they can learn when not to bite at all and learn that they should not bite too hard. This is called bite inhibition and it teaches puppies to control their jaws, even when they are in stressful situations.

Puppies learn bite inhibition naturally from their littermates and their mother. While playing, if a puppy bites another too hard, then the bitten puppy will squeal and run away. Hence, all the fun will stop and the puppy will have no one else to play with for the time being. If a puppy bites its mother too hard, then the mother will simply get up and walk away and hence its meal would have gone away with the mother too. All these natural occurrences serve as means of teaching a puppy when it is okay to bite and the amount of force that should be used in the bite that is acceptable to others.

It is best to allow a puppy to stay with its mother for at least ten weeks after birth. This way, he would have learnt some bite inhibition from its mother and siblings and so teaching bite inhibition will be a much easier task for you. Even then, more lessons of bite inhibition will still have to be given because a puppy has to learn that the human skin is much more delicate than the fur of its littermates.

Hand feeding your puppy is a great way to get your puppy used to having hands near its mouth and is also a great way to teach bite inhibition. If your puppy bites while you are hand feeding him, simply take away the hand with the food and squeal so that he knows that he has hurt you then continue feeding him again and repeat the exercise if he bites again.

You should also socialize with your puppy as much as possible, so that he gets used to gentle pulls on his ears, hugs etc and learns to tolerate these actions without biting. You should also consider giving him a treat after he undergoes these cuddly actions, so that he associates them with treats and looks forward to them. By doing this, you are conditioning his mind to expect treats when he is cuddled or gets a gentle pull on the ears instead of wanting to give a bite.

When training your dog for bite inhibition, you need to teach him to bite with little force and to bite less frequently. If you are playing and your pup bites you, simply say "ouch" calmly then walk away and give him no attention whatsoever. Repeat this exercise until the pup learns that hard bites are associated with you taking his attention away. Be patient, as this may take some time for the puppy to fully grasp but be constant in your methods.

You should also consider investing in a lot of chewable toys for your puppies to chew. You can redirect them to these toys, especially during the pup's teething stage, when he needs to bite something to make his gums feel better.

Chewing Everything

Another common problem observed by many dog owners is the constant chewing problem. Sometimes, dogs will chew almost everything and during this process, they destroy a lot of valuable items as well. Worse still, the dogs may end up chewing on something that is dangerous to their health and may become ill or even die as a result.

Most dogs chew because they are bored, they want attention, their behaviour is fear-related, they suffer from separation anxiety or they were not taught what not to chew and what can be chewed as a puppy.

Therefore, to curb the problem of constant gnawing, you have to find out what the main cause of his constant chewing is and then take necessary steps to fix the problem.

Teach your dog or puppy what he can and cannot chew from very early on and help him along the way by keeping all the things you do not want him to chew completely out of his reach. Therefore, if you don't want him to chew your shoes or clothing, keep them off of the floor. Do not confuse your dog by giving him toys that cannot be distinguished from common household goods. Hence, don't give him a sock or shoe to play with and then expect him to know the difference between his play sock or shoe and yours. Give him enticing chewable toys that he will like and try to use them as much as possible during playtime to get your dog to love them.

You can also coat some of your household items that your dog loves to chew on with a taste deterrent, such as Bitter Apple. This will make the items less appealing to your dog but remember that you have to reapply a fresh coating regularly to maintain its effectiveness.

You should also give your dog plenty of mental and physical exercises to keep him from getting bored. The amount of exercise that he gets should be determined by his health, age and breed characteristics. Therefore, give him plenty of walks around the block and give him some free time to play and release all that pent up energy.

Separation Anxiety

Separation anxiety can be described as a situation where your dog is very afraid of being left alone. Some pet owners confuse separation anxiety with boredom but these two are not the same. Although both often result to pawing, chewing and digging, separation anxiety begins as a panic as soon as you leave. The symptoms of separation anxiety include the destructive behaviours described above, as well as defecating or urinating inside (even when he has been properly trained not to do so), attempting to escape a room and even hurting himself in the process, persistent and intense pacing, excessive panting and constant whining, howling or barking. All the symptoms above only occur when you are away or when you are preparing to leave.

To reduce separation anxiety, you should try to not make such a big deal when you are about to leave home. This way, you are effectively telling the dog that leaving is a natural part of life and it should not cause such a commotion.

You should also practise leaving your dog for extended periods to lessen his separation anxiety. You would have to start small, by leaving for five minutes at a time and then gradually increasing that time until you can leave your dog for hours without the hysterics.

You can also take your dog out for walks before you go away. That way, when you do leave, he'll be tired and wanting to rest and therefore less aware of the fact that you are gone. You could also consider leaving things for him to do in your absence. Try hiding his favourite treats all over the room that you leave him in; it is his duty to search them out and find them. Also, leave him with his favourite toys so that he can have a ball to have fun with while you are away and therefore not focus so much on your absence.

You should also try leaving him in a room where he is less likely to cause harm or even hurt himself while you are away.

In some cases, you might need to use drugs especially if your pet does not become less anxious after trying everything we have talked about. You will have to speak to your veterinarian if you feel you will need one of these drugs for your dog.

Bonus Tips:

*Training your dog can require the aid of a lot of dog treats. This could put your dog's health in jeopardy. Opt to use regular dog food (different brand than what you feed him regularly) rather than treats; most dogs won't be able to tell the difference.

*Remember to decrease your dog's daily food intake when training to accommodate all the "treats" you will be giving him/her.

*This may be self-explanatory, but I cannot stress the importance of training the dog while it's a puppy. This is where habits are born and it is a crucial time for learning. Actions such as brushing your dog's teeth (crucial for optimum dental health) should begin routinely when the dog is just a puppy. This will abolish the fear most dog's have when being introduced to a toothbrush for the first time as mature dogs. Other good habits to build to eliminate any possible future fears in your dog are: brushing fur, clipping nails, holding and cuddling, playing with other puppies, interacting with humans and not giving the dog human food (especially during dinner time as this will lead to begging).

*Investing in your dog's present health will lead to never receiving an atrocious medical bill in the future. Buy your dog healthy food, with real protein and less fillers. Keep dogs (especially small breeds) warm during the winter months with a jacket; this will help prevent getting sick. Brush your dog's teeth routinely; vets say 85% of canines over age 4 have some sort of gum disease. Routinely check your dog for bumps, cuts or any abnormalities to catch potential problems arising in the early stages.

*Don't be afraid to let your puppy play with other dogs and run around. Dogs need to be dogs, even if you have a little teacup Chihuahua. Keep in mind that if you baby your puppy, it will most certainly develop bad behavior such as separation anxiety, over-protective, stranger aggression, barking and biting.

Conclusion

Thank you again for purchasing this book!

I hope that this book has helped you to understand how you can start dealing with some of those annoying behaviors that your dog has.

(First day I got my dog, Simba)

Finally, if you enjoyed this book, please share your thoughts and post a review on Amazon!

Thank you and good luck!

Printed in Great Britain
by Amazon